THE WORK OF HEROES: FIRST RESPONDERS IN ACTION

PARAMEDICS

to the RESC

by Nancy White

Consultant: Paul A. Werfel, MS, NREMT-P
Director, Paramedic Program
Assistant Professor of Clinical Emergency Medicin
Stony Brook University

BEARPORT
PUBLISHING

Credits

Cover and Title Page, Mike Powell/Stone/Getty Images; TOC, © Corbis/SuperStock; 4, © John T. Fowler; 5, © AP Photo/ Herman Bustamante; 6T, © Marka/SuperStock; 6B, © David L. Moore/Alamy; 7, © Monkey Business Images/Shutterstock; 8, © Juice Images/Alamy; 9T, © moodboard/SuperStock; 9B, © Monkey Business Images/Shutterstock; 10, © B. Christopher/ Alamy; 11T, Courtesy of the City of Miami Department of Fire-Rescue; 11B, Courtesy of the City of Miami Department of Fire-Rescue; 12, © Ron Thompson/St. Petersburg Times/Rapport Press; 13, © Brad Luttrell/Commercial Appeal/Landov; 14, © AP Photo/Columbus Dispatch/Renee Sauer; 15, © Robyn Beck/AFP/Getty Images; 16L, © Stockbroker/SuperStock; 16R, © Karin Hildebrand/Alamy; 17T, © Marvin Joseph/The Washington Post/Getty Images; 17B, © AP Photo/Reed Saxon; 18, © Fotosearch/SuperStock; 19, © Jaime Lopez/Los Angeles County Sheriff's Department; 20, © Damon Winter/The New York Times/Redux; 21, © ZUMA Press/Newscom; 22, © Steven James Silva/Reuters/Landov; 23, © Gabe Kirchheimer/Black Star/Newscom; 24, © ANT Photo Library/Photo Researchers, Inc.; 25L, © Robert Gallagher/Aurora Photos/Alamy; 25R, © AP Photo/Wilfredo Lee; 26, © David R. Frazier Photolibrary, Inc./Photo Researchers, Inc.; 27, © Ed Kashi/VII; 28T, © Exactostock/ SuperStock; 28B, © Margo Harrison/Shutterstock; 29T, © Exactostock/Superstock; 29ML, © Julie Dermansky/Photo Researchers, Inc.; 29MC, © AP Photo/Reed Saxon; 29MR, © Imagebroker/SuperStock; 29BL, © Exactostock/SuperStock; 29BR, © Paul Burns/Digital Vision/Getty Images; 31, © Leonid Smirnov/Shutterstock; 32, © Rob Wilson/Shutterstock.

Publisher: Kenn Goin
Senior Editor: Lisa Wiseman
Creative Director: Spencer Brinker
Photo Researcher: Mary Fran Loftus
Design: Debrah Kaiser

Library of Congress Cataloging-in-Publication Data

White, Nancy, 1942-
  Paramedics to the rescue / by Nancy White ; consultant, Paul A. Werfel.
    p. cm. — (The work of heroes: First responders in action)
  Includes bibliographical references and index.
  ISBN-13: 978-1-61772-282-0 (library binding)
  ISBN-10: 1-61772-282-0 (library binding)
  1. Allied health personnel—Juvenile literature. 2. First responders—Juvenile literature. I. Title.
  R697.A4W47 2012
  616.02'5—dc22

                    2011010391

For more information, write to Bearport Publishing Company, Inc., 45 West 21st Street, Suite 3B, New York, New York 10010. Printed in the United States of America in North Mankato, Minnesota.

071511
042711CGD

10 9 8 7 6 5 4 3 2 1

CONTENTS CONTENTS CONTENTS CO

Life in Danger!

In 2002, on a chilly February afternoon in Pittsburgh, Pennsylvania, a third-grader named Katlynn got off the school bus as usual and began her walk home. Almost immediately, she was hit by a school minivan. Her small body was tossed 100 feet (30 m) before landing. She was left on the ground **unconscious** and struggling to breathe. Her skin began to take on a grayish color.

 If a person's skin color looks gray and he or she is not breathing, immediate medical treatment is necessary. Without it, a person could die in the time it takes to get him or her to the hospital.

Ted Zeigler, a paramedic, happened to be driving along the same street where Katlynn had been hit. When he saw the accident, he stopped his car, jumped out, and rushed to the scene. That's when he noticed Katlynn lying in the street not breathing. Fortunately, Ted, who was off duty at the time, had his **paramedic bag** with him. He immediately took out a tube called an **oral airway** and inserted it into her mouth so the girl could breath. Would Ted be able to save Katlynn's life and get her to a hospital? Or was it already too late?

When people are hurt in accidents, paramedics help them before they get to the hospital.

Saving a Life

A few minutes later, Ted's paramedic partner, Mike Rogers, arrived by ambulance. By that time, thanks to Ted's quick use of the oral airway, Katlynn's color was back to normal. Ted and Mike carefully placed her onto a special device called a **spinal board**. Then the paramedics lifted Katlynn into the ambulance and rushed her to the hospital.

This patient was placed on a spinal board to keep her injured body completely still. Any movement could cause her further injuries.

An ambulance with paramedics inside racing down a street

At the emergency room, or ER, the doctors took over. They found that Katlynn's injuries included a broken leg, skull **fractures**, bruises to her brain and lungs, and liver damage. She was in **critical** condition, but she would survive. However, without the treatment she had received from Ted and Mike, she might not have even made it to the hospital alive!

 In 2002, Tom Murphy, then mayor of Pittsburgh, honored Ted Zeigler and Mike Rogers in a ceremony for their outstanding service in helping to save Katlynn's life.

Once an ambulance arrives at a hospital, the doctors take over after the paramedics give them a full report on the patient.

What Is a Paramedic?

Like all paramedics, Ted and Mike's job is to give immediate, life-saving treatment to patients *before* they get to a hospital. The patients they treat may have been seriously injured in accidents involving vehicles, as Katlynn had been. Or they may be people who have fallen and hurt themselves, have had heart attacks, been poisoned, bitten by an animal, or burned in a fire.

These paramedics are giving medical treatment to a patient before taking him to the hospital.

While paramedics are not doctors or nurses, they are trained to do many of the jobs that doctors and nurses perform. For example, they can give **intravenous** medications, **administer** oxygen to people who are having trouble breathing, restart a person's heart with electric shocks, and help women during childbirth.

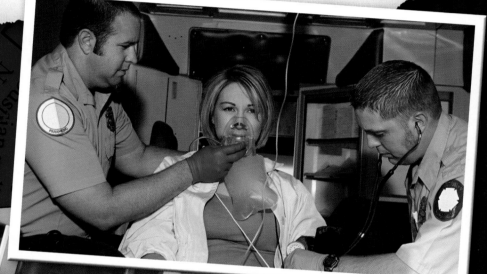

Paramedics continue to treat patients in the ambulance on the way to the hospital.

 A paramedic is a type of emergency medical technician (EMT). EMTs are trained to provide basic first aid to accident **victims** and transport them to the nearest hospitals. Paramedics have more emergency medical training than any other kind of EMT.

Paramedic Pioneers

Paramedics save thousands of lives each year. Surprisingly, however, there were no paramedics until the 1960s. While ambulances were used to transport patients to hospitals, the drivers were not qualified to give medical care. This situation was dangerous for the victims. By 1965, Dr. J. Frank Pantridge, from Belfast, Ireland, had discovered that many people died within one hour of a heart attack—often in an ambulance on the way to the hospital. In order to prevent this from happening, Dr. Pantridge developed the **portable defibrillator**. He also came up with the idea of having doctors ride in ambulances to provide medical treatment on the way to the hospital.

This is an example of an ambulance used in the 1950s, before paramedics helped transport patients.

Soon the idea of doctors in ambulances caught on in the United States. However, there weren't enough doctors to ride in every ambulance. The Miami, Florida, fire department came up with a solution to this problem. They had their firefighters learn medical skills and ride in ambulances. These firefighters were the first American paramedics.

 In 1964, Dr. Eugene Nagel, of Miami, Florida, wanted to prove that people other than doctors could treat patients. He lay down on the desk in his office and allowed firefighters, who were medically trained, to place a breathing tube down his throat.

Dr. Eugene Nagel (middle) tests some equipment for the Miami Fire Department.

The first paramedic teams in Miami, Florida

Paramedics in Training

Today, many firefighters are trained as paramedics. However, a person doesn't have to be a firefighter in order to become a paramedic. Though they may vary from state to state, the general requirements for being accepted into a paramedic training program are: 1) be at least 18 years old and a **certified** EMT, and 2) be **proficient** in reading and math.

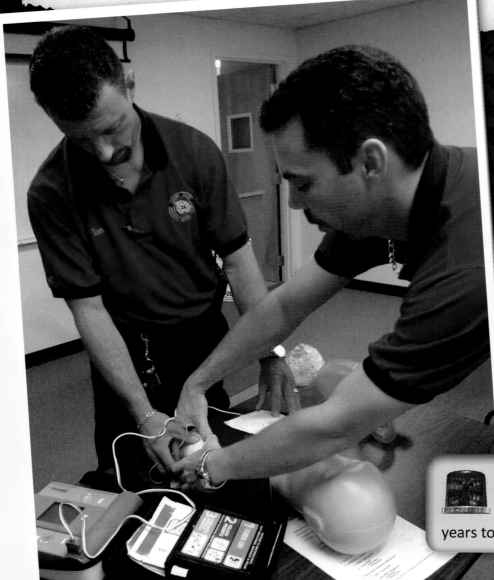

Students practice using medical equipment on dummies in the classroom before using the equipment in real emergencies.

Most paramedic training programs take one to two years to complete.

Paramedic training can start in several places—a classroom in a hospital, at a college, or at a technical school. During training, students learn how to **assess** what kind of emergency care is necessary, how to give medical treatment to patients with different kinds of injuries, and how to use special medical equipment. They also have to pass several tests that show they are brave and **mentally** and physically fit.

Beyond the Classroom

Classroom training is important, but it is only the first step to becoming a paramedic. After completing their class work, students continue their training in an actual ER, and on an ambulance, where real-life emergencies are happening every day.

Doctors work on a patient in an emergency room.

In the emergency room of a hospital, students watch doctors and nurses handle and treat patients. An ER handles a wide range of emergencies, and this experience helps prepare students for any type of situation that they may encounter on the job.

Outside the hospital, they ride in ambulances along with experienced, skilled paramedics. They watch and help the paramedics so that they will know what to do when they are out handling emergencies on their own.

A paramedic going through a simulation exercise

During training, students participate in **simulation**, or playacting, exercises. They pretend they are involved in an accident and take turns playing "victims" and "rescuers." They may even use special makeup so that it seems as if they are really bleeding or wounded. After the exercise is over, the students discuss how they handled the situation with their teachers.

Teaming Up

Once students have completed their training, they are ready to work as paramedics. Before they get started, they are paired up with another paramedic. Working in pairs is necessary because it usually takes two people to treat a patient and move him or her into an ambulance. Once in the ambulance, one partner stays in the back to care for the patient, while the other one drives to the hospital.

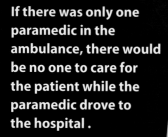

If there was only one paramedic in the ambulance, there would be no one to care for the patient while the paramedic drove to the hospital .

Paramedic partners are actually part of a larger team that includes the doctors and nurses in the emergency room at a hospital. By two-way radio, telephone, or computer, the paramedics report the patient's condition from the ambulance to the ER. The doctors and nurses then give the paramedics advice and instructions on how to care for the patient on the way to the ER.

This paramedic is using a computer in the ambulance to communicate with doctors and nurses in the ER.

A 911 **dispatcher** is also part of a paramedic team. Dispatchers answer the calls of people who have dialed 911 because they have been involved in an accident or other emergency. The dispatcher takes the caller's information—including the kind of emergency and location—and then contacts the paramedics by radio or phone.

A 911 dispatcher at work

Flight for Life

Sometimes paramedics have to team up with other rescue workers to get to emergencies that are tough to reach. For example, on February 7, 2011, paramedics had to join forces with the Los Angeles County Fire Department's Air-5 helicopter crew. Using a helicopter was the only way to reach a 22-year-old bicyclist who had crashed and fallen 250 feet (76 m) into a mountain **ravine**.

The accident took place along Glendora Mountain Road in the San Gabriel Mountains.

In order to save the bicyclist, the helicopter crew lowered two paramedics down by rope to where the injured man lay. When they reached him, they provided medical treatment, and then strapped him onto a **stretcher** that was **hoisted** up into the helicopter. As the stretcher was raised into the air by a rope, one of the paramedics hung from it to protect the injured man until he was brought safely inside. It wasn't long before the patient was taken to a nearby hospital, where he was treated for back injuries and broken ribs. Fortunately, the patient survived.

The injured man had called 911 on his cell phone at 10:10 A.M. Often, cell phones don't work in mountainous areas, so he was fortunate that his call went through. The rescue helicopter arrived by 10:45 A.M.

High winds made the rescue even more dangerous by blowing the stretcher into a tree as it was being raised up into the air.

Search and Rescue

Sometimes the most important part of a paramedic's job is finding people who have been injured. In a major natural disaster, such as an earthquake, people may be buried under collapsed buildings. That's why groups of paramedics from around the world were sent to Haiti when a huge earthquake destroyed the country's capital city on January 12, 2010.

paramedics' rescue work
iti was made even more
cult by the damage done to
s, vehicles, and hospitals.

The paramedics, along with **search-and-rescue dogs**, went looking for people who were buried under destroyed buildings. The dogs first sniffed out the victims. After a dog identified an area where a survivor was buried, paramedics inserted a tiny camera into the rubble to find the person's exact location. Once the person was found, paramedics could go to work digging out the survivor and giving him or her necessary emergency treatment.

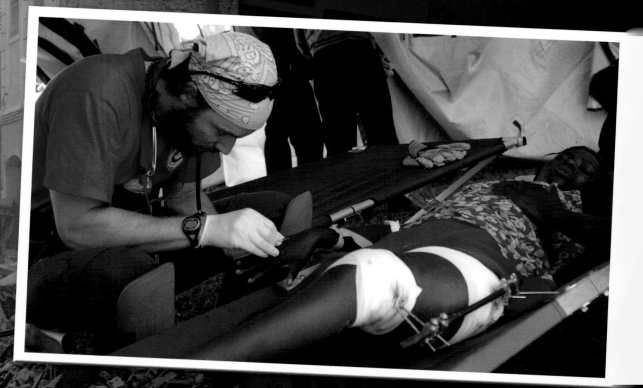

A woman receives medical care from a paramedic after the earthquake in Haiti.

 Paramedics, doctors, and nurses came from all over the world to help survivors of the earthquake in Haiti.

Helping the Helpers

When terrorists attacked the World Trade Center in New York City on September 11, 2001, flames and smoke poured from the twin towers. It wasn't long before both of the 110-story buildings collapsed. Injured people were everywhere. Fortunately, paramedics were there to help.

The World Trade Center after being attacked by terrorists

One of them was Lisa Desena. Her job was to set up a first-aid station near the collapsed buildings. While firefighters and police officers looked for injured people, Lisa stayed at her station, waiting for the wounded to be brought to her. Most of the victims had been injured by falling **debris**. Some were seriously burned or suffering from **dehydration** or **smoke inhalation**. Many of the people Lisa helped that day were police officers, firefighters, and paramedics—the very first responders who were on the scene to help others.

A paramedic cares for an injured firefighter after the collapse of the twin towers.

During a major disaster, an important part of a paramedic's job is **triage**. This is when paramedics assess whose injuries are the most serious and who needs to be treated first.

Snakebite!

On the same day that terrorists attacked the World Trade Center in New York, a 911 call came in from Lawrence van Sertima, in Miami, Florida. Lawrence had been bitten by a taipan—a deadly, **venomous** snake. Paramedics Al Cruz and Ernie Jillson got the call and rushed to the scene. They took Lawrence to a hospital, where he received special medication for the snakebite. However, the hospital didn't have enough of the medicine. Without more of it, Lawrence would die. The only place to get the medicine was from a zoo in San Diego, California—more than 2,000 miles (3,219 km) away!

Taipan snakes can grow to be more than 10 feet (3 m) in length.

The medicine that Lawrence van Sertima needed to survive is d **antivenin**. It is made the venom of a snake.

Because of the attack on the World Trade Center earlier that day, no planes were allowed to fly anywhere in the United States, except for certain government aircraft. However, Al Cruz was able to convince government officials to allow a plane to bring the needed medicine from San Diego to Florida. "The reason I am here today is because of Al Cruz," Lawrence later said.

Both Al Cruz (right) and Ernie Jillson (left) are paramedics with the Miami-Dade Fire Rescue Department. They specialize in saving snakebite victims.

Paramedic Pros and Cons

Being a paramedic is hard work. Unlike some other types of jobs, it can be very dangerous. Also, emergencies can happen at any time or place, so many paramedics have to work at night or outdoors in bad weather. In addition, it's possible to catch diseases from patients who are ill. Perhaps hardest of all, paramedics have to deal with people who are in pain and who may even die.

Paramedics often have to give medical treatment to people in the dark, using a flashlight.

Even though a paramedic's job is not easy, most paramedics enjoy their work. One reason is that they find it exciting— paramedics never know what kind of emergency they will be called out on next. Perhaps the most important reason they like their work, however, is that they get great satisfaction from helping people. They often reach people in terrible trouble whom they save from almost certain death. As a result, they have the chance to be heroes every single day.

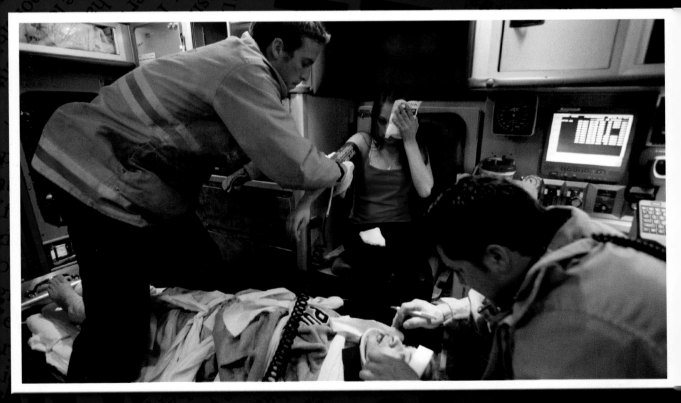

Sometimes paramedics have to treat more than one patient at a time.

 In **rural** areas and in many small towns, paramedics and other EMTs are **volunteers**. They work without being paid because they know how important it is to help people in need.

Paramedics' Gear

Paramedics use special equipment to move patients safely from the scene of an accident to an ambulance to an ER, without causing additional injuries. Here is some of their gear.

If a patient's neck is injured or broken, a *cervical collar* holds the neck in place.

If a patient has a head injury, a *head immobilizer* is used to keep the person's head from moving.

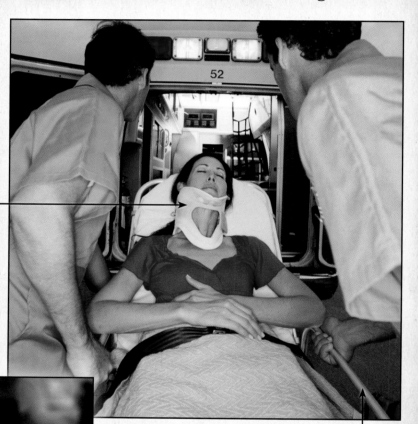

A *gurney* is a bed on wheels. It is **collapsible**, so that it easily fits into an ambulance.

A *spinal board* is used to carry a patient from one place to another.

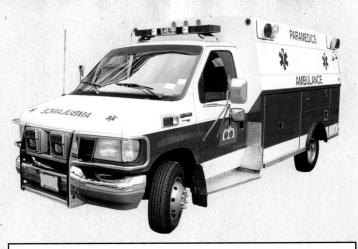

An *ambulance* is like an emergency room on wheels. Ambulances have to carry much of the same equipment found in an ER. This special equipment is used to monitor and treat patients on their way to a hospital.

An *EKG* (*electrocardiogram*) machine monitors a patient's heartbeat.

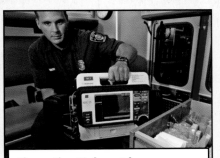

If a patient's heart has stopped, a *defibrillator* can start it beating again by giving the patient electric shocks.

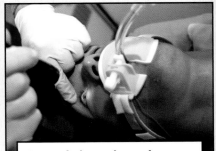

An *oral airway* is a tube that is inserted into an unconscious person's throat to help him or her breathe.

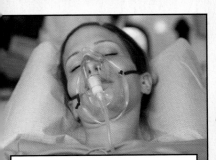

A *paramedic bag* is one of the most important pieces of equipment a paramedic carries. It contains everything from bandages, scissors, and a stethoscope, to a special tool for cutting seat belts to get injured people out of car wrecks.

An *oxygen mask* is placed over a patient's nose and mouth to help the patient breathe. Oxygen is pumped into the patient's lungs through the mask.

Glossary

administer (ad-MIN-uh-stur) to give something to someone

antivenin (*an*-tee-VEN-in) a medicine that blocks the effects of venom

assess (uh-SESS) to determine or decide

certified (SUR-tuh-fyed) having met the official requirements to do a specific job

collapsible (kuh-LAPS-uh-buhl) able to easily fold

critical (KRIT-uh-kuhl) dangerous or serious

debris (duh-BREE) scattered pieces of buildings or other objects that have been destroyed by an earthquake

dehydration (*dee*-hye-DRAY-shuhn) the condition of not having enough water in a person's body

dispatcher (diss-PACH-ur) an operator who sends out people, usually in vehicles, to help others

fractures (FRAK-churz) breaks or cracks, especially in bones

hoisted (HOIST-id) lifted up something heavy into the air with a rope or cable

intravenous (*in*-truh-VEE-nuhss) injected directly into a person's vein

mentally (MEN-tuhl-ee) having to do with the mind

oral airway (OR-uhl AIR-way) a medical tool that is put into an unconscious person's mouth in order to prevent the person's tongue from blocking his or her breathing

paramedic bag (*pa*-ruh-MED-ik BAG) a bag that a paramedic carries that contains first-aid tools

portable defibrillator (POR-tuh-buhl dee-FIB-ruh-lay-tur) a small machine that is used on a patient whose heart has stopped beating; the machine, which can be carried easily, gives off electric shocks to help a person's heart start beating again

proficient (pruh-FISH-uhnt) able to do something skillfully

ravine (ruh-VEEN) a deep, narrow space between two cliffs, hills, or mountains

rural (RUR-uhl) having to do with the countryside

search-and-rescue dogs (SURCH-AND-RES-kyoo DAWGZ) dogs that look for survivors after a disaster such as an earthquake

simulation (*sim*-yoo-LAY-shuhn) the act of pretending or imitating

smoke inhalation (SMOHK *in*-huh-LAY-shuhn) filling the lungs with smoke so that not enough air can get in

spinal board (SPINE-uhl BORD) a device that provides support to a patient with spine or limb injuries as he or she is moved from one location to another

stretcher (STRECH-ur) a device used for carrying a sick or injured person

triage (tree-AHZH) a system of deciding in what order sick or injured people will be treated

unconscious (uhn-KON-shuhss) not awake; not able to see, feel, or think, often as the result of a serious illness or accident

venomous (VEN-uhm-uhss) able to attack with a poisonous bite

victims (VIK-tuhmz) people who are hurt or killed, in an accident or disaster

volunteers (*vol*-uhn-TIHRZ) people who help others for free

Bibliography

Canning, Pater. *Paramedic on the Front Lines of Medicine.* New York: Ivy Books (1998).

Canning, Peter. *Rescue 471: A Paramedic's Stories.* New York: Ballantine Books (2000).

Kerins, Devin. *EMS: The Job of Your Life.* Poughkeepsie, NY: Vivisphere Publishing (2002).

Thiesen, Donna, and Dary Matera. *Angels of Emergency: Rescue Stories from America's Paramedics and EMTs.* New York: HarperCollins (1996).

Read More

Nickerson, Randy. *Quick! How Do You Dial 911?* Denton, TX: Tattersall Publishing (2001).

Silverstone, Michael. *Paramedics to the Rescue.* Bloomington, MN: Red Brick Learning (2005).

Learn More Online

To learn more about paramedics, visit
www.bearportpublishing.com/TheWorkofHeroes

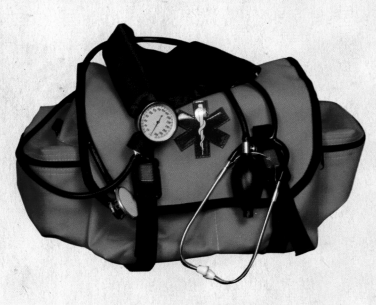

Index

About the Author

Nancy White has written many nonfiction books for children. She lives
just north of New York City, in the Hudson River Valley.

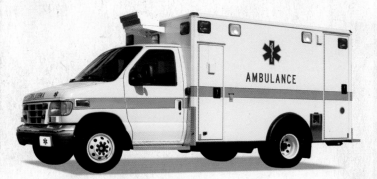